MIND YOUR

OWN BUSINESS

Focusing On Your Dreams

Written by - Emmanuel Arko-Dadzie

I will like to applaud you for investing in yourself, seeking knowledge and direct guidance in becoming a better version of you. We are all aware that knowledge is power, but knowledge is only power when it is applied. As you read this book of guidance, you will gain a mindset of a successful person. I ask one thing of you though. Take every piece of wisdom and information in this book serious and you will witness a major change in your life.

CONTENTS

ACKNOWLEDGEMENTS

This book would not have been made possible without the influence of very prominent individuals in my life. The individuals I have mentioned will not expect to receive such gratitude which is reflective in their meek-like behavior. The famous quote by Vladimir Lenin "show me your friends, and I will tell you who you are" will be evident as I give you a brief description of the individuals who have positively influenced me. Following this powerful quote, I am honored to show my utmost gratitude to the following individuals. I would like to begin by thanking my mentor and good friend Bill Daly. Bill has been an instrumental figure in shaping my mental wellbeing and has influenced my decisions in becoming a better man. Through aligning myself with Bill, I have learned the key secret to success is to remain honest with yourself to work hard in anything I set my mind on. My respect for Bill and a description of his character can only be understood by meeting the man himself. I would like to also show my appreciation to my close friend and brother Michael, popularly known as Big Mike. Michael has a character which projects peace, loyalty, and enthusiasm. Once you have a friend like Big Mike, rest assured you have a friend for life. My good friend and role model Yoma has been instrumental in enabling me to maintain focus when it comes to entrepreneurship and striving for success. Yoma has always been entrepreneurial, which encourages me to maintain focus on developing myself. Growing up in an Estate in London with young ambitious, stubborn and persevering individuals, Logan Riga throughout the years has become a positive influence, and a brother to me. Logan has enabled me to become fearless in pursuing my goals and has influenced my mindset in taking accountability with everything that happens to me and for me.

Throughout my working career, there are many individuals who have taken the responsibility of ensuring I remain focused and consistent. I have been known for my ability to network with people who are exceptionally gifted and relentlessly hard-working within their expertise. Before I take a drop of credit, I am honoured and humbled to acknowledge Jane James. Jane has been a mentor and guardian to me for many years. She provided me with the ability to re-learn the true secret to success and progression within the corporate environment. Through one of Jane's Programme The Real Apprentice, now known as Growing Talent, I was able to understand what it takes to stand out within the corporate world. Jane's patience and passion for giving back was the backbone and engine to my progression within the corporate environment. I have nothing but respect and love for Jane. Following my entrance into the corporate environment, Johanna Corllete, my mentor and a good friend has embraced me with warm arms. Johanna has dedicated her time to ensure I remain focused and ambitious in my endeavours. The work ethic, respect, and dedication of someone I inaudibly look up to and admire, David Cantillon is one individual whom I strive to emulate. David has a peaceful presence, unavoidably a hard worker who has gained respect and adoration within his field of work. I am privileged to have come across such a gentleman. My growth during University would not have been possible without the influence and love given to me through my aunt Evelyne, Grandma Tina, and my brother David Ansah. These individuals have been a pillar in playing a key role in guiding me to the right path and encouraging me to acknowledge my potential. My love for them is endless and my best wishes go out to them and anyone lucky to have an encounter with them.

Last but not least. The love and unity of my family, my mother, and father, and my two siblings Henry and Shennell, has been the backbone and inspiration which forms the engine enabling me to strive for success and self-development. The love of my mother is instilled in me so much so I have no choice but to honour her in every decision I make. My father, a role model, leader, a respected individual amongst his peers and community is an individual I look up to. His ability and passion for learning and self-development have been genetically passed on to me and my siblings. My father is a humble person who has a strong sense of self-respect and faith in God. His contribution to the church and passion for giving back is inaudibly praised.

Chapter One
MIND YOUR OWN BUSINESS

As the man in the silver Bentley GT Continental drove past the store, two young men in their twenties began to talk under their breath, "who does he think he is in that rental car?" The two men looked at each other as if it was a taboo to drive such a luxury car. Moreover, how did they know it was rented?

Such jealousies are secretly hidden in the hearts of many individuals. It becomes a form of comfort for those who have low self-esteem and need to boost their ego. As you carefully read this book, I ask that you open your mind and adopt an attitude of admiration and appreciation towards life. Forget about what you do not have and focus on the fact that you can get whatever you want. If you do not know what you want, you cannot get anything. But since you have the natural feeling of envy, you at least know what you will love to have.

We may not realise it but minding our own business is a way of showing respect to ourselves. Our ambitions and future success require our full attention. We all would like to achieve some level of success. But this can only be achieved once we give ourselves enough attention. Pity the man or woman who finds it entertaining to gossip about others' achievements or faults. This book will, without a doubt, save you from one of the most toxic forms of distraction that causes failure. This book provides vital explanations on the mindset of jealous people; people who do not mind their own business. People who spend most of their time talking about others. It will enable you to identify traits you were never aware of, causing you to procrastinate, judge others, and doubt your ability to become successful.

"Whenever you want to achieve something, keep your eyes open, concentrate, and make sure you

know exactly what it is you want. No one can hit their target with their eyes closed.

Paulo Coelho

We are all guilty of participating in an endless conversation, debating and discussing our expert opinions on how well-renowned celebrities, athletes, or entrepreneurs could earn more money or avoid some sort of failure or embarrassment. Although these successful individuals are surrounded by expert dieticians, accountants, advisors from every avenue, we are often enticed to voice our opinion on what caused their failures and what they need to do to maintain their level of success. We find ourselves in groups, enthusiastically debating with colleagues and friends on why footballers (soccer players) are paid so much money whilst keeping a close eye on their day to day activities and business transactions. We have fantasy online forums where we are able to decide which player we will buy and invest in, and our reasons on why they are the best choice for prospects. You are probably wondering what my ranting is all about. The core notion of this book will be gradually established in a way you will relate to. Rather than expressing an opinion or a common issue we all possess, this book will enable you to identify the benefits of minding our own business.

Now, the title of this book may seem abrupt to some of you and controversial to some. This, in my opinion, is wonderful news since the book aims to challenge our way of thinking and approaching things. When we hear the phrase "Mind Your Own Business," we often associate it with an egotistic character; uneducated and sometimes plain rude. Do yourselves a favor and disregard every notion you have attached to the phrase so you can have an open mind and truly grasp the idea that is presented to you in this short but direct piece. Once you have eradicated every possible notion you may have had with the phrase, I want you to see "Mind Your Own Business" simply as a piece of advice. Picture someone you admire and trust giving you this beautiful advice, saying Sarah or James 'mind your own business'. The reason we perceive this phrase as a negative gesture, is it's often voiced by an irritated individual. Taking out the behavior or mood attributed to the phrase, the term is really a key component to success. Most of us find it difficult loving ourselves and making our wellbeing a priority. Some may say it can't be so, after all, humans are extremely selfish. Most of us claim to love ourselves and want the best for ourselves, but we also know that talk is cheap and action speaks louder than words. When you look around you and at the lifestyle individuals live, daily, it is very difficult to see the self-love in it. Our actions do not match our words. We promise ourselves we will never smoke again or eat the wrong types of food, yet we find it difficult to avoid the naughty meal or nicotine sensation. We promise ourselves we will never do the negative things done to us by others, yet we end up repeating the same actions and blaming it on our past. There are many reasons we do these things which are investigated by many psychology researchers and institutions. As human beings, we are very complex and gifted in so many ways, however, we lack the concentration and focus to acknowledge these gifts instilled in us, simply because we do not—you guessed it—mind our own business.

We all have an inkling urge to participate in conversations about others, whether good or bad. We often state that we do not participate in gossip, however, paying mind to a gossiper and reacting with laughter is a form of encouragement which adds fuel to the fire. The topic of gossip is one that has been present for thousands of years. It has even been written in ancient holy books, discouraging and disposing of those who participate in gossip. According to the Bible, Eve was approached by a serpent who was depicted as the devil. The serpent did not come to frighten Eve but came to gossip and spread confusion in the mind of Eve so it could get to Adam. You notice the serpent did not come with facts about the forbidden fruit but began gossiping about the fruit. The definition of gossip according to Collin Dictionary is "unconstrained conversation or reports about someone or something, often involving details which are not supported by facts." Simply put, gossiping involves opinions explained as though they were facts. We've all been victims of gossip whether we are aware of it or not. It's a part of human behavior which subconsciously influences our behavior. Gossiping has become a form of conversation and is, at times, used to gain the attention of a party. Have you ever begun a conversation with the sentence "have you heard?" Once you begin a conversation with "have you heard?" you notice the party listening will suddenly be attentive and give you their full attention. What's the harm in gossiping? The reason why gossiping is a major deterrent to becoming successful is the effect it has on your mindset and reputation. A gossiper will have many listeners but will lack the respect and trust of their listeners. Think about this for a second. Would you trust or respect someone who always has something to say about others, particularly in a negative connotation? My guess is no! It is difficult for a gossiper to regain trust in a community or group once they've been defined by their conversations.

Participating in gossip is detrimental to your reputation. Although you may seem popular amongst your peers, you are often secretly despised. A gossiper gradually loses the ability to convince anyone genuine because their words are not facts. In a business case scenario or working environment, gossipers are merely entertainers and are not depicted as individuals with solid facts. This will affect opportunities which may arise in their department or industry. Most entrepreneurs, and managers at your workplace value honesty and individuals who are team players. Being known for gossiping will paint you as an unproductive individual who focuses primarily on others. A gossiper simply does not mind their own business because they are busy minding others. A gossiper will likely miss the opportunity to become a manager at a firm or be trusted in the long term with any sort of managerial position. For a gossiper to repair his reputation, he or she will have to avoid communication with peer groups who are actively involved on a day to day basis. If the individual still resides in the friendship of his or her current peers, it will bring about a bitter and tense atmosphere. A change in character will merely be seen as a desperate move to regain the trust of others. Furthermore, associates or "friends" who have a fixed perception of you will be the most difficult to convince. An individual who finds refuge in gossiping focuses primarily on the weakness of others or downplays the achievement and strength of an individual. Finding time to discuss another individual's success or failure, means you have not put aside enough time to find your own strengths and weaknesses.

Let us now take a look at the motivation behind gossiping and the benefits of it. When an individual is gossiping about another person, without factual evidence or good intention, the main aim is to discredit that individual. You must now consider why they would go so far to discredit that individual. Each of us have weaknesses we must work on, and taking time out of our day to speak negatively of another individual is a show of low self-esteem. Gossip is derived from jealousy. You will not go out of your way to speak negatively about another individual's weaknesses or achievements if you did not have any type of envy or negative wishes towards them.

A long term detrimental effect of jealousy which we often ignore is the perceived self-worth of an individual. Being jealous of someone merely demonstrates you believe you're not able to attain the wealth or skills they possess. It's an acceptance of self-defeat and unwillingness to strive to achieve the same goal. Jealousy is a word we usually don't want to be associated with. It is referred to as an emotion derived from a sense of low self, fear, and anger at oneself. We often mistake jealousy for envy, as they are closely related. However, they are separate in meaning; the difference between a jealous person and someone who envies others is the mindset behind the feeling. Collins Dictionary defines the word jealous as 'suspicious or fearful of being displaced by a rival'. Collins Dictionary's' definition for envy is 'a feeling of grudging or somewhat admiring discontent aroused by the dispossession, achievements, or qualities of another'. Analysing the difference between being jealous and envious, you notice it has a slightly different mindset to it. A jealous individual tends to have a sense of hatred or anger towards an individual whilst an individual who envies another wish they were in the other person's shoes. Someone who envies you could also admire you. An envious person may focus their energy on becoming the person they envy whilst a jealous person simply hates the individual and doesn't really want to know how that person became successful.

I remember, at my University; there was a clever fellow who seemed to know the answers to every question. He was always right, and the lecturers favored him amongst others. Charlie was never aiming to make us look bad or suck up to the lecturers. He was simply more intelligent than us all, more importantly, he put in more study time than any of us. He was always willing to help anyone who asked for help and seemed serious. However, some liked him and envied his intelligence whilst others hated him because he made them look bad.

We all have a little jealousy and envy instilled in us. However, we decide whether the feeling is one which will encourage us to do more or seek advice. We do not know the root of true jealousy but we do know we have a choice to allow it to motivate us or make us complacent. The mindset of a jealous individual will not allow them to achieve much, as they focus all their energy on analysing others. The time they use to look at other individuals' success could be used to ask for advice and begin their own journey of personal success.

Jealousy clouds your mind in ways you will not consciously witness. This brings me to a crucial point regarding silent death gradually caused by jealousy. With an increase in social media usage and acceptance, the urge to portray your daily life as a living movie and something exciting in order to gain virtual or distant followers constantly increases. This has been the cause of many mental health issues which has led to individuals taking their own life. We are all guilty of thinking we are not selfish or jealous individuals until we are constantly presented with images and videos reflecting the life of those who claim to be wealthy. Images and videos of a beach-view villa followed by the hashtag "living my best life" will certainly make you define the lifestyle you live. I'm not pointing fingers at social media, but it benefits you to understand the progressive but subtle effects of the various factors that form the layers of a jealous mindset.

The personal effects of jealousy can be detrimental to the body and mind to the point it becomes the downfall of an individual. So many negative circumstances that happen to us have been accepted as part of life and simply ignored. Jealousy is one form of illness that does not only affect us directly in the long run but affects the people around us, especially the ones we love. The ones we love and are close to will be around us more often than those we just associate with. A jealous individual will focus primarily on the negative and will likely cause friction amongst their peers, knowingly or unknowingly. Friendship is maintained through trust and sacrifice for one another. If a group of friends envy one another, it creates a negative competitive environment which only distracts them from the friendship. A jealous person has no loyalty towards anyone but themselves, which could result in loneliness. The reason this is a major issue, points to the contradiction correlating with jealousy and the need for maintaining a social class. Jealous people feel that possession of an item which they have not earned or been gifted with will put them in a happy place or mood. The danger of having such a mindset is, it makes you fail to identify the true reason for others' happiness.

The pressing question now is, what if a jealous individual wants something intangible? Within your group of friends, you will notice there are differences in the skills or talent each individual possess. Some friends "just have it." They seem to be great at everything they do. They always seem happy and never complain about their life. You then have a friend who always complains and moans about their life and how bad it is. For some reason, everything they attempt to do seems to fail and they will not hesitate to explain to you in detail how their life is set up for failure. A jealous individual who dreams of obtaining a natural talent or skill earned by a friend who works day and night to perfect their craft will begin to breed hate and negativity. This individual dreams of the day when you fail and give up on your dreams so they can feel better about themselves. They will be the first to spread rumors about you to divide your group of friends.

Chapter Two
THE PEOPLE AROUND YOU

"If I have seen further, it's by standing on the shoulders of giants"

Carefully selecting the people we surround ourselves with is, in my opinion, the most important advice of all. I'm not advising we leave our lives in the hands of others, but we must carefully place ourselves in the company of people with ambition. It is funny because the title of the book is "Mind Your Own Business." Some may say, 'how can you mind your own business if you are trying to get into others'." This title does not promote loneliness and does not advise us to become an island. Rather, it signifies the importance of focusing on our own personal goals and how we may achieve them. It literally gives you the key to awareness and success. Standing on the shoulders of giants signifies a sense of humility and wisdom. We often use the saying, 'survival of the fittest,' but we do not explain the strategy used by the fittest. The fittest are the ones who are able to extend their success and knowledge to gain wisdom throughout the process of learning. They are the ones who are hungry for information on how to mind their own business and become successful. A mentor by the name of Patrick Reid once advised me when I began my new work to open my eyes and learn as much as I can at work and in the future when I start my own business use it. Patrick explained that I can do more if I ask questions and be inquisitive. What Patrick was signifying correlates with the saying, 'mind your own business' by seeking to develop yourself. The aim is to develop yourself, and by surrounding yourself with the right people, you will begin the journey of success. Patrick and his wife Claudine have been a great source of inspiration to me although they hardly see me. But the lifestyle they live, the time they give to people, and the humble spirit they possess around individuals make it easy for anyone to approach and learn from them.

We've heard the quote 'birds of a feather flock together.' This quote is very true yet difficult to digest at times. To explain my reason for such a claim, let us analyse the quote. We know that the people we surround ourselves with have an influence on our lifestyle and can change our mindset. But then we also surround ourselves with people of low self-esteem in order to feel good about ourselves. The problem with this is the fact that it's also a sign of pride and low self-esteem. We all have friends who seem to underachieve either in academics or personal talent. However, because they choose to remain our friends and are loyal to us, it does not mean we should get rid of them. The quote, I believe, describes people who are not encouraging or have no form of loyalty to you. These people are the ones who use their friends and have no input in their journey to success. There are those who also take from others but do not give back. Some of these friends will only call you when they are in need but they disappear when you need them.

Now we have identified a few characteristics of friendship, let us look at a few behavioral patterns we should seek for within a friend. It is very essential, and I repeat, very essential that we have friends with different characteristics. The reason for this is simply because everyone has different values that will eventually benefit you. The first and most important friend you must have is the 'action man' or woman. This friend talks less but does more. The action friend is a person who will tell you they will do something and call you the next day to say it is done. A good friend of mine at University, Yoma, always spoke about the business he will create and his plans for the next five years. The next day or so, Yoma would call to show me what he has accomplished. This got me out of my seat and I thought to myself 'what am I doing sitting down watching TV.'

The positive effect this had on me was great. I wanted to be able to tell him what I had accomplished when I next meet him. Apparently, we spend, at least, four to eight hours a day talking about what we are going to do and daydreaming rather than getting to business and doing them. It is funny when I and my siblings are talking about what we 'plan' to do and how it will help us in the long run, and we suddenly stop talking and say something like "I'm talking too much let me just do it." So, analyse your friends this week and be closer to the ones who are actively pursuing their dreams.

The second type of friend you must have is 'the encourager' and 'motivator.' These friends may not have accomplished a lot but have strong positive attitude towards their goals. They always make an effort to encourage others, and their mindset is very encouraging. Be careful not to select a friend who is encouraging but also discouraging. These friends cannot be trusted as their mood always changes. The encourager also has a bit of an action attitude but more motivating. They are the ones you can call when you feel down and you'll be sure to get motivated at the end of a phone call. Be sure to keep these types of friends very close because you will need their inspiration when you feel like giving up. I always thought personal trainers were useless and did not add any value to my workout. However, there are times when you want to give up running or lifting weights and you cannot mentally do your last push. This is when the personal trainer will encourage you and suddenly, you are able to lift one or two more reps of weights or run another mile on the treadmill.

The third type of friend you must have is 'the good listener.' Good listeners are very important because they have a sense of compassion and understanding of what you go through and tell them. Individuals with many friends are the ones who are good listeners. They are trusted by many people and allow others to let go of any burden they may have. Another reason to have a good listener around is, you may have an idea for a business or plan for how you will become successful. You can then go to or call your trusted good listener and express your thoughts to which they may provide valuable insight into your ideas.

The fourth type of friend you must have is 'the entertainer' or 'funny guy/girl.' These individuals make life more interesting and exciting. Their sense of humor and ability to make you laugh and smile is vital to our development. As we go about our daily routines we experience various challenges which make us feel down and consider giving up. However, a little cheering up and laughter would lead you back to focusing on your goals. This may sound funny, but there will be a time when you do not want to be motivated. You want to vent and express your feelings, whether negative or positive; you just want to express yourself. This is when the 'funny friend' comes into place. Their sense of humor and ability to make you laugh will be powerful in restoring your enthusiasm and passion for your goals.

The fifth and final type of individual you must surround yourself with is the 'confident individual'. In every group, there must be, at least, one confident person who can defend the group and possibly lead them. The confident individual may appear to be cocky or arrogant but their leadership attributes and boldness will be great value to you. A very good friend of mine, Logan, is an example of a confident individual. I knew him to be a fearless individual. Once Logan puts his mind into anything, he will do whatever it takes to achieve it. He once went into a well-known clothing store with no work experience and managed to convince the manager to employ him. He later moved to France for a few years by himself and accomplished his goals there before coming back to London. The influence he had and is still having on me is valuable to my self-development. Let us remember, we are not talking about imitating the attributes and characteristics of the people we surround ourselves with. These five close friends of ours are 'minding their own businesses.' So, all you are doing now is surrounding yourself with these friends who will be the key to influencing your behavior and self-development.

Chapter Three
MOTIVATIONAL CONFERENCES

Motivational conferences and events can be very positive and essential in building one's self-esteem and self-belief. Their aim is to enable individuals to believe they can achieve something they always thought was difficult or impossible. I've been to various motivational events and have left the venue thinking "yes this is my year." Most modern places of worship have adopted the teachings and methods of motivational conferences. Adopting their methods has generated a vast amount of income and followers for them. Individuals have actually sold their precious possessions in order to afford payments for some renowned conferences. Pumped up and ready to achieve greatness, these individuals go home assured in their minds that they would definitely make it. Bear in mind that I am totally not against motivational conferences as they provide an essential aspect of developing the mindset for greatness and success. However, it is worrying when individuals go home feeling pumped up only to realise after a month or years, that they are still in the same position. To make it worse, the money they invested in motivating themselves will not end up back in their pockets. The blame here is both on the individuals and the hosts of the conference; however, we should take responsibility for our own decisions.

Now, to the interesting part of motivational conferences, and a more positive outlook on their events. I will never forget a conference I went to, titled Rich Dad, Poor Dad by Robert Kiyosaki. An associate of Robert was hosting the conference. He made sure to motivate and inspire us to achieve greatness, but most importantly, he provided us with ideas on how we could increase our wealth and become financially free.

His realistic and straightforward approach was, to me, the best way to truly inspire wealth building. One thing which still inspires me till this day was when he asked the audience "who wants a free copy of the book?" We all started jumping up and down trying to get his attention like little kids. Everyone including myself, my brother, and my father stretched our hands and waved it in order to catch his attention. To our surprise, after minutes of shouting and waving, someone in the audience stood up and walked to the speaker and took the book off his hands. The speaker then said to us, "this woman will lead in life and will become successful because she takes actions and does not wait for someone to give her anything." Whilst we were all begging and trying to get the speaker's attention, she took the bold action and went to get what she wanted, which was a great lesson for me. Others may have been upset that they did not think of getting up and getting the book, but it was a blessing in disguise. Now, there will be a time when we have to wait for what we want, but it does not eliminate the fact that we must take action to get them.

Let us briefly focus on the three most important reasons you should attend an inspirational conference and the mindset you should have when going to these conferences. The main purpose individuals usually have when going to a motivational conference is to be inspired to achieve greatness. They take notes on quotes which will temporarily motivate them but forget to note down step-by-step methods to actually achieve their own personal goals. Others go to these events out of desperation, not inspiration, or are forced to attend by a friend or relative. The most important and only reason you should go to a motivational conference is to network. Now, some of you may be confused at how that could be the only reason. I'll give you a great reason why this should be your only purpose for attending such conferences. If your reason for paying a fee of £30 or £50,000—no matter the cost—for inspiration when you can be inspired for free on YouTube by subscribing to motivational online conferences where you receive the same information or more, then you are making a bad investment. If you really want to achieve success, you need to have a bigger plan than paying to be inspired. You need to network with people with the same vision or people who have achieved success. You can then keep in contact with these individuals and be constantly fed with information and inspiration on how to achieve your personal goals. That's when your investment for these events is worth it.

The topic of motivation is widely popular across all genres and have been the source of many acclaimed success stories and charitable organisations. Without motivation, many revolutionary movements may not have been possible. Motivation is, in my opinion, the most potent internal force which enables an individual to act physically. Motivation has no moral grounds in its purest form. To explain further, let's recollect tragic times when an individual with powerful leadership skills used motivation to persuade a large group of individuals to endorse and contribute to disastrous ideas. On the other hand, motivation has been a great tool for inspiring life-changing ideas and projects, and most importantly, has been the pillar for encouraging a positive mental attitude towards life and individual goals. Our accomplishments are aligned with our goals and the motivation behind those goals, so it is essential that we pay attention to what inspires us. When we discuss motivation, it is important that we understand the correlation between that and our surroundings. Motivation does not suddenly appear and randomly stores itself in your mind. That said, most individuals who have ambition and goals are often unaware of the source of their motivation. We are all influenced by something; be it subconscious or conscious. These things govern our mindset to form an obsession which becomes motivation. It is safe to say that motivation is not an option, although, a lack of effort is often described as a lack of motivation. To enlighten you to understand my reason for stating that motivation is not an option, we must first understand the definition of motivation. Motivation is described as a reason or reasons for acting or behaving in a particular way. So, the notion that motivation only refers to a positive outcome or mindset is completely out of the window. Now, as previously mentioned, motivation is often influenced by your environment and surroundings, so if you are constantly surrounded by individuals who all aspire to be athletes, you are more likely to be motivated to pursue an athletic career or record. We've heard the saying, "show me your friends and I'll tell you your future." There is truth to this, although there are rare occasions where an individual somehow is different from his or her peers and ends up becoming the successful individual amongst the group.

Motivation tends to be effective at a certain point of an individual's life and is not always welcomed depending on their current mind-frame. Have you ever been so down and uninspired, and suddenly your jumpy cheerful friend tries to be positive and motivational. This can make things worse in the sense that you may even doubt yourself further and go into a state of depression. Motivation itself is beneficial, but where you get it from and why you get it is very important. Let's take a look at the individual who seeks or finds motivation at a time of frustration. This individual will "do whatever it takes" to exit their current situation and make things better. Now, there are two things likely to occur. Number one: the individual will begin to work harder, seek advice, eventually change his or her life, and more importantly, maintain the work ethic learned in the process. Number two: the individual will begin to do whatever it takes to be in a better position. But, as soon as the work overload and intensity is felt, they will give a great excuse for why they failed or gave up on achieving their goals. In both scenarios, both individual were motivated but achieved different outcomes. The need for hope and a better future constantly renews the necessity for motivation. This has given birth to many religious organisations and motivational speakers.

When you feel the need for motivation, it is very essential to ask yourself these questions. Am I desperate for change or do I just want my current problem diminished? One of my favorite statements by Jim Rohn is "we only change for two reasons, and two reasons only, inspiration or desperation." Sometimes, a desperate individual will achieve faster results but will they maintain the momentum? An inspired individual may take a longer time to learn how to become successful, and will likely keep progressing no matter their achievements. Now let's look at the words "want" and "need." If you want something, you may do some work to achieve or attain that thing. Whereas if you need it, you are more likely to do what it takes to attain or achieve that thing. However, to embed the reality of success in you, you will need to get used to achieving your goals and not see it as a need or desperation move. Learn to accept success and what it takes to achieve it as a 'normal' characteristic. The wealthy one percent accomplish and attain what they want not what they need. They have built a natural tendency for achieving their goals. They see something they want and they find a way to attain it or learn from someone who has already attained it. This does not apply to those without basic necessities such as food, water, and shelter. This strongly applies to individuals who are comfortable with their basic needs and want to aim higher in life and accomplish whatever they choose to. There are events where homeless individuals have been able to turn their lives around and become multi-millionaires. So, imagine the mindset that an individual had and still has to maintain their wealth. Jim Rohn, rest in peace, who is still my favorite speaker of all time said, "if someone gives you a million dollars, you better become a millionaire fast so you get to keep the money." Read this one more time and understand the concept of that statement. Having physical possession of a million dollars or pounds does not mean you, as an individual, are a millionaire. What happens once you begin spending the money? You no longer are a millionaire. But if you have an idea of what to do with the money and the right people to console, you are more likely to remain a millionaire and even become a multi-millionaire in the process.

When talking about motivation, the word "feeling" is often used without much attention. Wake up, it's time to go to the gym, 'but I'm not feeling it today.' Stop eating that extra cheese pepperoni pizza and have a salad like you said you would, 'ah but I'm not feeling it today.' Hey Lucy, did you hear about the promotion coming up? Apparently, they've put your name forward. Lucy: "I have a good feeling about this."

Feelings, feelings, feelings! Ask yourself right now, "how do I feel?" Have you gone through a crazy day at work or had an argument with a loved one or do you simply feel stuck in your current state? Please highlight this or write it somewhere safe. Feelings are illusions! That's it! They are not bad nor are they good. They are simply a confirmation of our mind trying to protect us. You see someone from afar, you have no idea who they are or what they do, but as they approach, you get a 'feeling' about them. You may be completely wrong but your feelings allow you to make a decision about the individual. Feelings dictate our mood which heavily influences our actions. You will realise at times that you feel happy and suddenly, you are down. This feeling is often not understood or investigated, we usually brush it off as just a feeling. Next time you feel this way, acknowledge your current surrounding or environment. Keep a mental note of whom you've spoken to in the past hour or the type of music you are currently listening to. We won't focus primarily on the things that cause us to have emotional feelings, but it is important you ask yourself these questions next time you're in a mood.

Chapter Four
ASSOCIATES, PARTNERS & FRIENDS

In this book, we spoke about the people around us and their influence on our well-being and mindset. This chapter will explain the three most important roles we need in our life to achieve success. These three roles will be supported with examples of the people I personally know and their influence on my well-being. Associates, partners, and friends are the most important tools we have in developing ourselves and inviting a great and positive mental attitude into our lives. But before they become valuable to us, we must understand them and learn to differentiate them from each other. Each role has its strengths and weaknesses, but bear in mind that you should only use them for their strengths and nothing more. There is no point in trying to force each role to do what they are not made to do; you will produce empty results. Before we begin to explore these roles, I urge you to make mental or physical notes on the roles and decide the individuals you believe will best suit them. By doing this, you will have a draft plan after understanding the roles and can begin working and achieving various goals immediately.

So, we begin with the role of an associate. An associate is someone you know through a transaction, whether constant or a one-off transaction. They could also be someone introduced to you by another individual who does business with that individual. Never make the mistake of classifying an associate as a friend or a partner. An associate does not have any personal ties with you apart from business or some sort of transaction. An associate could be a teacher, a business partner, a mentor, or someone you know from activities. That said, an associate could become a good friend and mentor in the long run. The important things to always remember when dealing with associates is the fact that they may consider themselves to be a friend or close to you outside their business dealings. This is not necessarily bad and could, at times, play an important role in developing a stronger relationship. The most important thing to bear in mind at this point of your relationship is to keep business as a priority and "friendship" as secondary. Remember, they are an associate for a reason and have no interest in you apart from doing business with you. Those who become too close to associates and eventually view them as friends could be in for a rude awakening. Although, this is possible and may happen often, building a strong friendship with an associate can distract you from your long-term goal or strategy. If such a relationship is organically built and is mutual, it could end up in many opportunities and success. We've heard stories of business associates who eventually became friends and have created companies together.

Associates can arguably be the most valuable source of a network when looking to start a business or rise up to high ranks in a particular field. The reason for this is due to the network each associate may have. Take it like this. You meet a friend of a friend who happens to be at the same venue as you. You initially introduce yourself as a friend of Michael for instance and explain your field of business. This, in turn, could lead to an investment, a partnership, or good business advice. In fact, if that certain individual has no experience in your field, they may guide you to someone who has. Interestingly enough, associates have the flexibility to play the role of an advisor, "friend," or a business partner. They often do not get attached to one particular character and are able to switch to a friend or business mindset, which is why you should not categorise them to one character or entirely be obsessed with being their friend. That said, you must ensure to keep your associates close to you and maintain respect amongst them because they will elevate you to opportunities you've never come across before. Maintaining a good relationship with your associates requires effort and vision. Your reason for maintaining a good relationship with your associates must be something of value. If your reason is simply to benefit from them, your relationship will soon grow sour and business with those individuals is likely to falter. Associates are often your greatest network system, as they are accustomed to working with many individuals across various fields of expertise and are often a source of a network to other ventures.

Keeping in contact with your associates is extremely important, I repeat, extremely important. If you do not maintain great communication with your associates, they will easily associate themselves with someone else or a different venture. Since an associate is not your friend and is often introduced through a project or a business partner, they can easily dispose of you. Maintaining good communication with them is vital if you wish to keep them within your network. A phone call once a week will be a great way to keep in contact. Inviting your associates to an event where they could meet new people is another great way of maintaining such relationships. Simple friendly gestures such as asking how their kids or loved ones are doing, or remembering a story they told you and catching up on it is an informal but powerful way to keep a good relationship with associates. As a practice, write down two associates you value the most and decide a day of the week that you will contact them or ask of them. This will keep you in their mind and will form a solid basis for opportunities.

Partnership in any tradition can be the most powerful force if strategically organised. However, it can also be the worst decision you have ever made. To partner is to combine energy, intelligence, finances, and more importantly, the workforce. This enables an individual or an organisation to double their results and explore many untapped ideas and opportunities. During a partnership, each individual will have to agree to the terms and conditions that each partner is legally obliged to. To form a united partnership with someone, there are many do's and don'ts to abide by.

Of the previous relationships, we mentioned throughout this chapter, a partnership type of relationship is a delicate one. To partner with someone is to risk your finance and vision with them. It requires both individuals to trust each other very much. Trust is the only true trait needed for a partnership to flourish. Without trust, a project or idea will not be successful since each member is not in unity with creativity and agreement.

In any relationship, a strong partner looks out for the other and is honest to the point where they admit their wrongs and acknowledge one another's weaknesses. Although this sounds like a romantic story, it's actually the cornerstone of a strong and lasting partnership even in the corporate world. Once trust is established, the second most essential trait you need in a partnership is value. Without value, there will be no point in partnering in the first place. Value without trust is suicide, but trust without value is also a financial suicide, so both go hand in hand. The value will determine the power you have in a partnership and the reputation you hold for many years to come. To add value to a partnership, you must be intentional in developing yourself. Self-development can only be obtained once you are honest with yourself. Know your weaknesses and your strengths, and work on them daily. The value you bring to your team, business, employees, or partner will motivate them and others to take their partnership seriously. The value of an employee will give that employee certain flexibility with an organisation, whereas an employee that is less valuable doesn't. Your value in an intimate relationship will determine how far your partner goes to please you. Without value, there is simply no point in the meeting. The third most important trait for a successful partnership is unity. Unity and trust have a lot in common, however, unity is a broad word which focuses on the mindset and vision of both party. If you are not unified in mindset, goal, or vision, the partnership will break apart or fall into dismay and confusion. You have to sing from the same hymn book, as they would say. As you progress with your partner, there will be differences in opinion or ideas, but understanding a major goal and agreeing to it is a great key to a successful partnership.

A partnership may, at times, not be for everyone. For example, if you are an individual who has great expectations and refuses to settle for anything, you may have to endure a long journey to finding success. This does not necessarily mean you should settle for anything, but simply encourages you to enjoy every stage you may find yourself in. By learning to appreciate every stage of your partnership, you learn more about yourself and your partner and you train yourself to possess a positive mental attitude.

Friends, friends, friends, what would we do without them? Without friends, the world would be a lonely place. Throughout this book, we disclosed the importance of friends and the different types of friends we need in order to be content. Let's discuss the importance of friends and a few tips on choosing the right friends. We all have friends who inspire us and those who simply make us happy. Selecting the right types of friends will enable you to remain hopeful and ambitious. The saying "birds of a feather, flock together" is crucial to this topic. If your friends always talk about going out and having fun every Friday night, you are more likely to be accustomed to such routine. You are likely to become like the five close friends you hang around with. The secret to achieving much in life is to choose new friends and being intentional with it. Once you choose the right circle of people, you will eventually reach a level of success that your circle is accustomed to. Achieving your goals will become normal and thinking with a positive mindset will be embedded in you.

Chapter Five
BECOMING GREAT IS A CHOICE

The beginning of this book we identified the various attitudes and characteristics of individuals with low self-esteem and no ambitions. These individuals tend to envy others and gossip about others' success. In the first paragraph, we witness a level of jealousy and judgment without any solid facts, when the two young men were speaking negatively about the man in the Bentley continental. This chapter aims to inspire you and provide an understanding of the mindset of successful people and illustrate, in-depth, how this mindset could be adopted to achieve our own personal greatness. As you read the quotes selected, I ask that you obtain an open mindset. See these quotes as valuable pearls which have proven to open the doors of immensity for many successful individuals. The only difference between the highly successful people and others with less success is the ability to have an open mind and the willingness to follow the advice given by great individuals.

> *"Be not afraid of greatness. Some are born great, some achieve greatness, and others have greatness thrust upon them."*
> William Shakespeare - Twelfth Night

William Shakespeare was a great English poet, writer, and actor. The quote above has the great inspiration behind it which will be explained very soon. Shakespeare's influence was so great that he was often called England's national poet and has been studied in many educational facilities across the world.

Now, let's dig deep into the quote from Shakespeare. "Be not afraid of greatness." This sounds very easy to say; however, this first part of the quote has a very deep meaning to it. The first question will be, why would anyone be afraid of greatness? Surprisingly enough, most people are more afraid of achieving greatness than not being successful. There are many reasons why this may be. As individuals, we are so used to our friends and family members telling us to be careful or to think through before we do anything. Such warnings and lack of risk-taking are what makes most of us afraid to achieve greatness or even attempt to do so. Another common reason why achieving greatness may be an issue for most people is the challenges it brings. Achieving greatness comes with many ups and downs, and most people will rather be comfortable and "secure" which is why they look for job security rather than money opportunities. Being great does not mean you have to forsake any form of security, whether it's working for someone or yourself. It only signifies that you think bigger and, more importantly, follow through your vision with massive action.

As Shakespeare explains, 'some are born great, some achieve greatness, and others have greatness thrust upon them.' This notion is true in the sense that some are genuinely talented from birth. You can see a six-year-old child doing things even adults cannot dream of doing. These prodigies are born with a gift which will take a century to acquire. Most individuals have to put in long hours and years of work in order to become as talented as others who are born with gifts. However, these individuals do not look at the fact that they do not have the natural gift, but they work at it until they become as great as the others or even greater. There is a saying that goes, "hard work beats talent if talent does not work hard enough." This is the right time to stop comparing yourself with others or being discouraged by others' natural gifts and start 'minding your own business.' Shakespeare was a human like all of us. He had the same needs we have. He died with a legacy. We have the chance right now to achieve greater things than he did. Let's rise up, stop daydreaming, and make things happen.

"Keep away from people who try to belittle your ambitions. Small people always do that, but the really great people make you feel that you, too, can be great."

Mark Twain

Mark Twain's quote is one of the most important quotes of all time because it addresses a major aspect of becoming successful. People influence us more than anything else, more than our circumstances. I say this because even if a person goes through a major downfall in their life, the people around them could either help them rise from the situation or fall further. Mark suggests that those people around us who often belittle you should be kept at a distance or removed from our lives. Think of it this way, if we really want to achieve greatness, then we must remove every form of negativity in our lives. This includes those who belittle us. These people think small and will discourage anyone who dares to think big. The main reason for this could be the fact that they are afraid you will fail or it could even be a form of jealousy towards you for even thinking to dream. Great people are not afraid of dreaming big and are often very encouraging to others who dare to dream. These people will go out of their way to help you move forward in whatever you are trying to achieve.

Before going further, the advice on achieving your goals will be to choose your friends carefully. Note down any friend or associate who often talks negatively about you or even themselves. You need to carefully consider if these friends are worth keeping around if they are always negative.

"Great spirits have always encountered violent opposition from mediocre minds."
Albert Einstein

As you dare to begin the journey of greatness and massive success, you will constantly arouse the spirit of jealousy and envy amongst many individuals. Surprisingly enough, the individuals you most need to be watchful of are your friends and relatives. These individuals may not intentionally aim to put you down or demotivate you, but they often do, as an act of low self-belief and fear. They wish to protect you in their shield of "safety" and often wish no harm to you. Now, the opposite could also occur, where individuals around you notice the level of effort and passion you have in accomplishing your goals and begin to fear that you may achieve them and be successful than they are. They will try their hardest to put fear into you so you consider giving up or changing plans. Beware of these people, because it is very hard to spot them since they cover their fear and jealousy in sheep's clothing. There are various ways you could spot such individuals. These techniques may not be justified by law, but they provide a very vital awareness of who has faith and good intentions for you, and those who do not. There are three strategies which are very simple but do not fully signify an individual's intentions, as an individual's main intention is hidden within their mind, covered by a cunning poker face. Strategy one: You must always ask individuals the same amount of questions about their life as they ask you. This is mirroring them to see their reaction and behavior. I will give you an example. Certain individuals are so eager to find out your ambitions and what you are up to, and when you ask them about theirs, they reply with a closed answer. If this occurs religiously, such individual is probably nosey or gossiping, which could lead to jealousy. On the other hand, they could just be feeding off your motivation, which I highly doubt. Strategy two: Always ask the people around you what they think about a certain idea you have. Make sure to not expose the true idea, as they may steal it or share it with others. hear their reply, be it positive or negative, and judge for yourself. Bear in mind that when it comes to ideas, negative opinions matter as much as positive ones. What you are looking for is feedback which criticises without providing reasons or tips. And the third strategy is to ASK FOR HELP! This is one of my favorite strategies. Help is one of the most powerful words made by man. It signifies the need for urgent attention. Now when you ask for help, those who love you and those who hate you will both come to the rescue, so do not judge your relations by who comes to your aid. As close relations and associates seek to help you, listen closely to their words and impressions. Some may say "remember I did this for you." Others may tell their friends how much they helped you. These individuals are boastful and cannot be trusted. They pride themselves in being greater than their peers and are a very bad company. You should stay far from them.

"Until you're ready to look foolish, you'll never have the possibility of being great."

Cher

This statement by Cher has a very powerful meaning to it if you carefully analyse it. It simply states that unless you are willing to make mistakes in public or secret, you will not be great. Now, remember, we are not talking about being rich here, but is great. Being great has a higher value than being rich. The reason is simply that a great person can rise after they fall because they have programmed their mind to do so. Whereas, a rich individual may fall and find it extremely hard to get back up on their feet because their mind is not transformed to deal with difficult times. In this age of pride and the increasing use of artificial lifestyles on social media, embarrassments or looking slightly incompetent has become a taboo. This has made it very difficult for people who are caught up in the trend to become great in whatever they choose to seek. Being selfless has its benefits in creating a solid foundation for achieving greatness. Not caring what people around you would say or what your status may end up becoming, will open doors of opportunities for you. Cher's statement demonstrates the trait many successful entrepreneurs possess. For example, Richard Branson, a well-known entrepreneur who is dyslexic is known as one of the wealthiest people on earth. Richard did not allow his dyslexia to judge his fate. He did not focus on what people around him may think of him, but rather decided to chase after his dreams; therefore encouraging many individuals who previously believed that being dyslexic is a barrier to success.

"The mark of a great man is one who knows when to set aside the important things in order to accomplish the vital ones."

Brandon Sanderson - The Alloy of Law

This quote is extremely relevant in every sense if you carefully pay attention to it. It speaks on the mark of a great man, which is a very important word to note down. Identifying the mark of great men is literally unfolding the blueprint for success. Brandon Sanderson provides us with one of the crucial traits or characteristics of a great man. As expressed, the mark of a great man is one who knows when to set aside important things in order to accomplish the vital ones. We all know that important things must be accomplished in order to progress in our daily goals and plans. They are often very difficult to ignore, especially when it involves letting others down. We may look at this quote and suggest that it is obvious. I mean, who wouldn't leave the important things to accomplish the vital ones? There have been talks about great leaders and people of influence who have cancelled important meetings and tasks in order to attend to their children or resolve certain issues they believe are vital.

But how do we classify something as important or vital? This can be decided with a simple self-questioning and mental prediction of scenarios. Now, the decisions you make or classify as vital may not always lead to the best results, but it must be done and never regretted. Let's create a scenario of a young woman named Melisa. Melissa has a job offer from a well-known retail store that is willing to give her a part-time or a full-time job. Melissa has finished her second year of University and needs income. Her friends are all driving and she's often unable to go shopping with them because she cannot afford the things they buy. However, Melissa's dream job of becoming a Lawyer at a well-known firm could be accomplished if she completes her final year at University. She now has to decide which more important to her. Taking the year of University to earn money will make her happy, as she can now go on holidays with her friends and do the things she always desired. Better yet, she could get the car she has wanted at the end of the year before going back to University. The important thing, in this case, could be the fact that she needs money for various things, essentially holidays and being able to buy certain items which will make her happy and fit amongst her peers. The vital thing in this situation will be to remain focused on the bigger picture and complete her studies as soon as possible in order to reap bigger results. This will not only be beneficial to her, but it will serve as a lesson and inspiration to all her friends.

FINAL WORDS

My dream is to be able to not only inspire you, the reader, to obtain the mindset of a successful person but to actually be successful. Great individuals—past and present—were given the golden rule of success which they took seriously and has resulted in their success. Sean Combs, also known as Diddy, always talks about love and happiness no matter how hard life is. This is essential because the mind controls our actions, and having a positive mindset will eventually flourish into an incredible success. You do not have to look far to find success, you only need to look around you and study the greats. Make it your goal to stop talking about the success of others in a spiteful way and learn to Mind Your Own Business.

The meaning of life is different for everyone, but we all want happiness. Happiness is a choice but a difficult choice to make. It is not linked to the possession of material items or the need for social awareness. Society has done a great job in determining that our happiness is linked to marketable products and social systems. However, once these social status or products are no longer valuable—or worst case scenario, taken away from you, you are then left to find the true meaning of happiness. The acceptance of life and the interesting things it brings will make you a happier individual. Choosing to be happy regardless of the issues you face is a powerful mindset to have. It allows you to build an internal filter which is not powered by external products or systems. When you feel a sense of regret, unhappiness or dissatisfaction, you can look deeper into yourself and tap into the inner peace you've always had. Items are just that, items. The power they hold is given by you and society. People feel good when they have money or drive the latest car because the value of that product is determined by society, which is good for business. However, the emotional attachment to the products is a major issue which often defines individuals.

The purpose of this chapter is to open your mind possible ideas on how to maintain your vision and plans. The reason why I have chosen to speak primarily on your vision and plan is the simple fact that our vision is useless without a solid and strategic plan to accomplish it. Every organisation, before they became global, had a clear vision and a plan on how they aimed to achieve its goals. The first step to every achievement is noting down your dream goals. Your dream goal is the fun part because you are allowed to have the wildest thoughts ever. Whether your ultimate dream in life is to become Mr. Universe or the first person to invent an idea which may be classified as crazy to people, it doesn't matter! At this stage, it is your choice to remain 'realistic' or innovative. But you must make your dream so valuable that it takes most of your attention. This dream must be your priority, more than going out with friends or playing online games.

Now that you have your goals figured out and are very passionate about your choice, it's time to search within and understand the true motive behind your visions. I'm not here to condemn you or preach that you must have a clear conscious and positive motive behind your vision. It's more rewarding and encouraging to have a long-term motive which serves as an encouragement and a lesson to those who read about your success in the future. We've seen it many times in movies, such as Scarface and American Gangster, that have become popular around the world. These movies explain how poverty and hardship can motivate an individual or a group of people to become wealthy, no matter the cost. Though, the motive behind the wealth tends to corrupt the minds of the individuals and make them forget why they wanted the wealth in the first place. This ends in hurting those you first worked hard for and spending your time and money on those you met along your journey of wealth.

Once you have achieved your goal, how will those achievements make you different or make you feel? There is no point in working hard and making major sacrifices if you will remain the same as a person. Fine, you may have acquired a level of financial wealth, but have you, as a person, become wealthy. Are you the wealth or have just acquired income? This is a very vital question you need to ask yourself during your daily effort in getting your goals accomplished. There are several multi-millionaires and billionaires who believed in self-development rather than money accumulation. These successful individuals have been in situations where they have lost everything including their homes due to bad business transactions and even lost their spouses. The ones who were able to bounce back and accumulate even more wealth are the individuals who developed themselves and made themselves mentally wealthy.

Now, you have read this interesting short book, I would like you to be a person of action and not of words. The greats have the same thing in common, and that is taking action. Taking action is the key to achieving anything. Pity the person who speaks many words and little action, for they will endure many wasted years and will regret in the long run. Do not be a man or woman of words but one of action. Do not waste your time speaking negatively about another's downfall or success, but spend your time being positive and saying encouraging words. Mind Your Own Business and success unfold upon your life.

25496521R00045

Printed in Great Britain
by Amazon